NORMAN WHITNEY

Paradise Island

HEINEMANN

PARADISE

North

West ← → East

South

AMOR

ISLAND

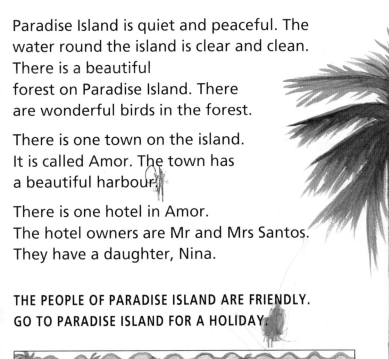

Paradise Island is quiet and peaceful. The
water round the island is clear and clean.
There is a beautiful
forest on Paradise Island. There
are wonderful birds in the forest.

There is one town on the island.
It is called Amor. The town has
a beautiful harbour.

There is one hotel in Amor.
The hotel owners are Mr and Mrs Santos.
They have a daughter, Nina.

**THE PEOPLE OF PARADISE ISLAND ARE FRIENDLY.
GO TO PARADISE ISLAND FOR A HOLIDAY.**

Hotel
Santos

CHEAP
ACCOMMODATION

FRESH
FOOD

TRADITIONAL
MUSIC

3

Tourists come by boat to Paradise Island.
They like the forests and the tropical birds.
They swim in the clear water.

Mr Santos welcomes tourists to his small
hotel. The tourists like Mr Santos and his
family.

The tourists eat delicious fresh food.
They dance to the music.

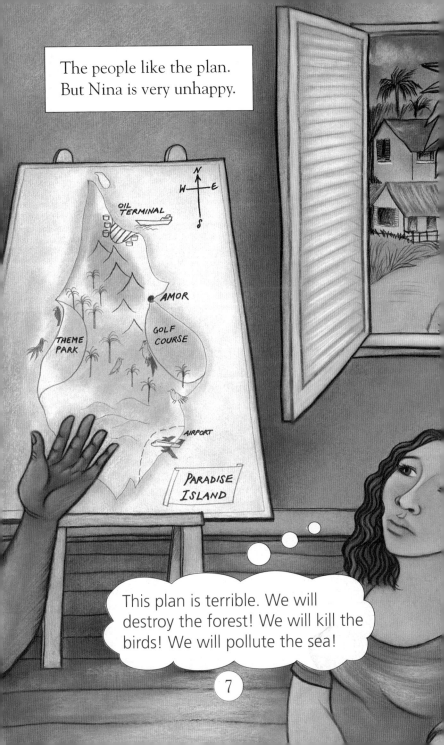

Many tourists come by plane to Paradise Island. They play golf. They visit the theme park.

The tourists spend a lot of money. They stay at the new Hotel Santos. They eat American burgers. They dance in the laser disco.

Mr Santos is very happy.

The people of Paradise Island hold another meeting.

'The tourists want better roads,' says Mr Santos. 'This is my new road plan.'

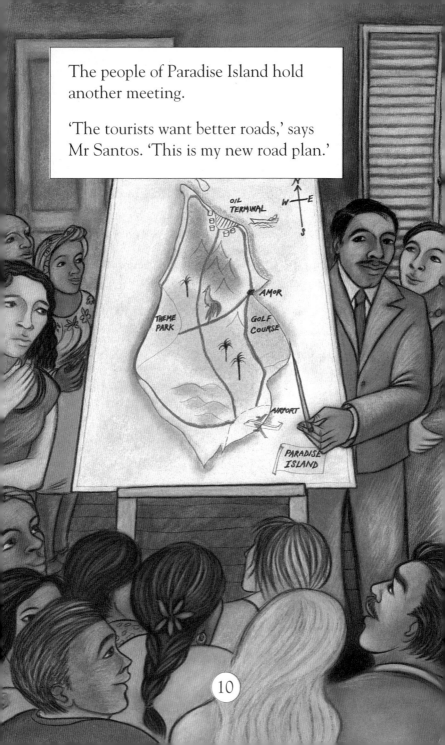

'The tourists want to see our tropical birds,' says Mr Santos. 'Here is my plan for a birdcage.'

Nina is very angry. She stands up and speaks.

Your plans are terrible. Those roads will destroy our island. That birdcage is cruel!

Nina! Be quiet! This is not your business!

Your father is right. You're young. You don't understand. Go home, Nina!

More tourists come to Paradise Island.
But they are not pleased.

'This island isn't quiet,' says one man.
'It's noisy.'

'The traffic is terrible,' says his wife.

'Paradise Island isn't beautiful,' says
a girl.

'It's ugly,' says her brother.

'Is this the forest?' says a woman with
a camera. 'Those birds look so sad!'

BAR
BURGERS
SUPER LASER DISCO
We don't like this new hotel. We don't like burgers. And we don't like discos.
The sea is dirty. There's a lot of oil pollution.
The islanders are not friendly. Everything is very expensive. I'm going to write to the Holiday Magazine.

Dear Holiday Magazine,

Do you remember your report about Paradise Island? Well, the island is very different now.

There are a lot of roads. And the traffic is terrible. The forest is dying. The tropical birds are kept in a cage. The sea is dirty and polluted.

The Hotel Santos is ugly. Everything is expensive. The people are not friendly.

Don't go to Paradise Island for a holiday!

14

We must save the forest. We must free the birds. We must stop the oil pollution.
We will cook fresh food. We will play our own music.
Yes, you're right Nina. I'm sorry.
PARADISE ISLAND
"A beautiful place for everything and everybody"
DIS CO
We must learn from our mistakes.
Nina, we're proud of you!